Animals in the

Monkey

by Mary Hoffman

A Random House PICTUREBACK®

First American Edition 1984. Text copyright © 1983 by Mary Hoffman. Text and illustrations in this form copyright © 1983 by Belitha Press. All rights reserved under International and Pan-American Copyright Conventions. Published in the United States by Random House, Inc., New York. Originally published in Great Britain by Belitha Press Ltd., London. *Library of Congress Cataloging in Publication Data:* Hoffman, Mary, [date]. Animals in the wild—monkey. (A Random House pictureback) SUMMARY: Briefly describes the physical characteristics, habits, and behavior of monkeys. 1. Monkeys—Juvenile literature. [1. Monkeys] I. Title. QL737.P9H68 1984 599.8′2 83-21158 ISBN: 0-394-86554-5
1 2 3 4 5 6 7 8 9 0
Manufactured in Italy by Sagdos

People live in families. Monkeys do too.
Monkeys are good parents. This squirrel monkey
is being cared for by its mother. But some
monkey babies are protected by their fathers.

A mother usually gives birth to one monkey at a time. A small baby clings to its mother's belly. As it grows older it travels on her back, like this young olive baboon from North Africa.

Monkeys spend a lot of time in trees. This capuchin
from South America has found something to eat.

Maybe it is a nut or some fruit. Or maybe
it is an insect or a bird's egg.

This macaque is catching crabs to eat. It lives on an island in Indonesia. It has to move very fast in the water to catch a crab.

This Japanese monkey is washing a potato before eating it. The little monkey watches. Monkeys are smart animals and learn from watching others.

All young monkeys learn to keep themselves clean.
They also help other monkeys stay clean. This is
called grooming. This adult male olive baboon is
being groomed by the other baboon. This gets rid
of dry skin and insects.

Monkeys all live in groups. Sometimes as many as
a hundred live together. The big male with the
silver mane is the leader of this group of
hamadryas baboons. Baboons have very complicated
rules for living together.

Although baboons live mainly on the ground, other monkeys live mostly in trees. They can do this because they are so good at climbing and balancing. These spider monkeys can hang just by their tails.

This baby woolly monkey is a good acrobat too.
How easily it hangs underneath this branch!
It takes time to learn to balance like this. The baby
chacma baboon on the next page still looks wobbly.

Monkeys need to look fierce sometimes. It is a way to help protect themselves from enemies. This mandrill looks very frightening with its sharp teeth and its striped, brightly colored face.

Even a very little monkey can look fierce.
This pygmy marmoset is the smallest of all the
monkeys. Full-grown pygmy marmosets are only
about eight inches long from head to tail.

There are more than thirty different kinds of
monkeys. One of the most colorful is the
golden lion marmoset. The golden lion father
is the one who carries the babies.

Here is a white-nosed monkey from Africa. It is easy to see how it got its name. Not all monkeys have such special markings. The entellus monkey on the next page is plainer but still beautiful.

Howler monkeys make loud noises when they
want to defend their homes or territories.
This howler is quiet at the moment. Howler
monkeys live in Central and South America.

This monkey is called a Goeldi's marmoset. It lives in South America too. Some South and Central American monkeys have a special tail that can grasp things. They use their tail like an extra hand.

This is a young proboscis monkey. It is named
for its big pink nose. Proboscis monkeys live
on the island of Borneo. They sunbathe in
treetops and eat leaves.

Rhesus monkeys live in India and other parts of
Asia. They are not afraid of people and sometimes
are pests. But rhesus monkeys are very important
to the Hindu people, who worship a monkey god.

Acknowledgments are due to Bruce Coleman Ltd.
for all photographs in this book with the
following exceptions: Jacana Ltd., cover, 14; 18–19.